To Jenny, for our own amazing age.
— *C. B.*

To Rita Painter and Rachel McInnes, two amazing library divas.
— *D. T.*

Text © 2015 Chris Barton
Illustrations © 2015 Don Tate

Published in 2015 by Eerdmans Books for Young Readers,
an imprint of Wm. B. Eerdmans Publishing Co.
2140 Oak Industrial Dr. NE
Grand Rapids, Michigan 49505
P.O. Box 163, Cambridge CB3 9PU U.K.

www.eerdmans.com/youngreaders

Manufactured at Tien Wah Press in Malaysia

20 19 18 17 16 15   4 5 6 7 8

The type on the front cover was handlettered by Don Tate.
The illustrations are mixed media, ink, and gouache on
watercolor paper.
The text type was set in Humanist Slabserif 712.

Photo of John Roy Lynch courtesy of the Archives and Records
Services Division, Mississippi Department of Archives and History.

Photos of Chris Barton and Don Tate provided by
Sam Bond Photography.

Library of Congress Cataloging-in-Publication Data

Barton, Chris.
The amazing age of John Roy Lynch / written by Chris Barton;
illustrated by Don Tate.
pages cm
Summary: "A picture book biography of John Roy Lynch,
one of the first African-Americans elected into the United States
Congress" — Provided by publisher.
Audience: Age 7 to 10.
Includes bibliographical references.
ISBN 978-0-8028-5379-0
1. Lynch, John Roy, 1847-1939 — Juvenile literature. 2. African
American legislators — Biography — Juvenile literature. 3. Legislators
— United States — Biography — Juvenile literature. 4. United States.
Congress. House — Biography — Juvenile literature. 5. Reconstruction
(U.S. history, 1865-1877) — Juvenile literature. 6. United States —
Politics and government — 1865-1900 — Juvenile literature. 7. African
American politicians — Mississippi — Biography — Juvenile literature.
8. Mississippi — Politics and government — 1865-1950 — Juvenile
literature. I. Tate, Don, illustrator. II. Title.

E664.L985B27 2015
328.73092 — dc23
[B]

2014018586

The Amazing Age of
JOHN ROY LYNCH

Written by
CHRIS BARTON

Illustrated by
DON TATE

Eerdmans Books for Young Readers

Grand Rapids, Michigan · Cambridge, U.K.

JOHN ROY LYNCH had an Irish father and an enslaved mother. By the law of the South before the Civil War, that made John Roy and his brother half Irish and all slave.

His father lacked the power to change the law — he was just an overseer, a hired hand. Besides, while he may have loved *these* slaves, he most likely took the whip to others.

But Patrick Lynch, it was said, had a plan — a plan to liberate Catherine and their children. The law would allow him to buy them. They would "belong" to him, but he could let them live as if they were free.

John Roy was just a toddler in 1849 when his father took sick and died. Pat Lynch left all he had, including his unfinished plan, to a friend named Deale. But Deale did not liberate Catherine, nor John Roy, nor William. Deale kept them enslaved and sold them to a new owner.

John Roy might have been free by the time he was two. But he was not. Precious time — years of would-be freedom — were lost.

John Roy's new owner, Mr. Davis, did not send him
out into the hot Louisiana cotton fields. Instead,
Mr. Davis kept John Roy at his big home across the
Mississippi River in the city of Natchez.

His job was to fan Mrs. Davis, serve her ice water, open the door of her carriage, and shoo the flies from her table. She must have thought he would be grateful for the privilege.

In Sunday school, John Roy's ears heard more than they were intended to. He noticed how Mrs. Davis twisted Scripture to encourage obedience to her and her husband. When they sang

> *To serve the present age,*
> *my calling to fulfill:*
> *oh, may it all my powers engage*
> *to do my master's will*

it was clear which "master" Mrs. Davis had in mind.

Mrs. Davis said she could not abide telling lies. She would boast of her own sister, who claimed never to have lied.

"What do you think of that?" Mr. Davis teased John Roy one day.

"I think she told a lie when she said that," he replied.

Full of rage and spite and hurt, Mrs. Davis banished John Roy from the big house on Homochitto Street. She sent him across the river to Tacony Plantation, to hard labor and swamp fever amid the cotton bolls.

She was not alone in rage and spite and hurt and lashing out. The leaders of the South reacted the same way to the election of a president — Abraham Lincoln — who was opposed to slavery. They quit the United States and formed their own country.

The Civil War had come. Mr. Davis and others in gray uniforms fought for *their* freedom to deny John Roy *his* freedom. Northerners in blue battled just to preserve the Union.

Then, to strengthen that Union, President Lincoln
declared that the slaves would be free.

FOR JOHN ROY, true emancipation came the summer he turned sixteen. It did not come from the president's pen, or even from the arrival of two hundred blue-clad men on horseback. It came instead when he sold a chicken for a dime to a Yankee soldier and bought himself a boat ride across the river back to Natchez.

Elsewhere, the war still raged. Here, for John Roy Lynch, it was the beginning of an amazing age.

First, he found a job. The four dollars he earned in one month as a waiter wasn't much. But it was four dollars more than he'd earned before. It was a start.

Searching for more satisfying work, he went from waiter to cook — ah, the freedom to make such a move! — then from cook to better-paid pantryman on board the *Altamont*, a Union transport steamer.

It was on the *Altamont* just after the war's end that
John Roy heard the news: President Lincoln was dead.
John Roy and the white sailors were united — united
with bowed heads, united with wet cheeks, united
with broken hearts.

When the *Altamont* chugged away, taking its crew home to the North, John Roy could have gone along. He had the choice to stay or go, and he chose to stay. Natchez was his home. Fellow former slaves reveled in the promises of freedom — family, faith, free labor, land, education. John Roy wanted to be part of that.

Freedom, however, soon turned sour. Mississippi whites passed laws to make Mississippi blacks into slaves under different names: "Apprentices." "Vagrants." "Convicts."

Under those laws, the fines and jail time were harsh for blacks who treated whites as equals, and harsher still for whites who treated blacks the same. And sometimes hate-filled whites dealt out penalties far worse than what the laws called for.

In too many ways, this new world of black and white was just like the old one.

But in another new world of black and white — photography — John Roy found opportunity. At seventeen he became the messenger for a local portrait shop, and he soon took on more responsibility.

Trusted to develop the photographs, John Roy continued
to develop himself. He took note of everything, every
detail of operating the shop. Because the shop owner had
John Roy Lynch, he didn't need anyone else. By nineteen,
John Roy was running the place by himself.

Across the alley behind the shop sat a public school for white children — close enough for John Roy to see the blackboard and hear the teacher through the windows. When the shop was quiet, John Roy went to class without setting foot outside.

At a night school taught by Northerners, John Roy learned to compose letters — simple at first, then elegant and soaring. He read in newspapers about how unhappy the victorious North was with the stunted freedoms in the South. John Roy knew that changes would be coming to Mississippi.

When those changes came in 1867, it meant black men would be able to vote. Not John Roy, though — he was still too young. All the same, he got involved in the Natchez Republican club, making speeches and stirring up support for a new Mississippi constitution.

And he began buying land. It hadn't been so long since John Roy had been forced to work someone else's land, but now he owned a piece of this earth for himself. John Roy bought more and more, including some property of his own on Homochitto Street.

GOVERNOR

General Adelbert Ames

In 1868 the U.S. government appointed a young Yankee general as governor of Mississippi. The whites who had been in charge were swept out of office. By river and by railroad, John Roy traveled to Jackson to hand Governor Ames a list of names to fill those positions in Natchez. After John Roy spoke grandly of each man's merits, the governor added another name to the list: John Roy Lynch, Justice of the Peace.

Justice. Peace. Black people saw reason to believe that these were now available to them. Just twenty-one, John Roy doubted that he could meet all those expectations. But he dove in and learned the law as fast as he could.

Justice of the Peace

John Roy Lynch

He settled disputes between servants and employers. He
corrected whites who assumed that the law still allowed
them to mistreat black people. He hitched young couples
in matrimony, then helped patch things up for those
same pairs. (And if the husbands mistakenly thought that
John Roy could send them to prison if they didn't shape
up, he let them keep right on thinking that.)

When Election Day came in just a few months' time, the people of Natchez elected John Roy to the Mississippi House of Representatives, to help govern the whole state. He gained the power to change the law.

Here and there around the state, whites tried to bully black voters away from the polls through whippings and beatings and threats. They didn't succeed, but they didn't give up either.

Clearly, there was work to do. And John Roy worked to make freedmen like himself truly free — not just in name alone, but full-fledged, fully educated citizens.

Mississippi's people as a whole were poorly educated. The state sorely needed new schools for black and white alike. But who would pay for those schools? And what would happen to the cotton with the field hands in a classroom?

The people elected leaders to answer those questions, and those leaders elected John Roy Lynch to lead *them*, as Speaker of the House. John Roy was only twenty-four years old, and he was still on the rise. In 1872, voters all the way over to the Alabama border and down to the Gulf of Mexico elected him to the United States House of Representatives.

It took several days for him to travel to Washington, D.C. The ten years since he'd been a teenage slave on Tacony Plantation had gone by almost as fast.

Too fast, for some.

U.S. Congressman or not, a black man could still find himself barred from certain hotels. But that wasn't the worst of it — not by far. Back home, white terrorists burned black schools and black churches. They armed themselves on Election Day to keep blacks away. They even committed murder.

In a way, the Civil War wasn't really over. The battling had not stopped. But white Northerners had grown weary, and the U.S. government wavered. Hard, hungry times came to the North, overshadowing injustice in the South. The decent people of Mississippi were not outnumbered, but they were outgunned and on their own.

John Roy held on, would not be silenced. This was not who America was, he said. Not who she should be. Not what she must become. On the floor of the United States House of Representatives, this half-Irish, all-American, democratically elected former slave spoke these words:

When every man, woman, and child can feel and know that his, her, and their rights are fully protected by the strong

arm of a generous
and grateful
Republic,
then we can
all truthfully
say that this
beautiful land
of ours, over which
the Star
Spangled Banner
so triumphantly waves,
is, in truth and in fact, the
"land of the free
and the home
of the brave."

If John Roy Lynch had lived a hundred years (and he nearly did), he would not have seen that come to pass. The years following his speech were filled with more disappointments, as whites continued to push back against the freedoms that blacks had gained.

But John Roy never forgot that the period of Reconstruction after the war had been an age of amazing promise and potential — and he insisted that others remember this too.

He continued to believe that the laws of this land could bring about justice. He continued to believe that the people of this land could bring about peace.

HISTORICAL NOTE

"Reconstruction" is the name for the dozen years following the Civil War, from 1865 to 1877. During those years, the United States struggled with how to treat the states that had seceded to create the Confederate States of America, and four million formerly enslaved people. Understanding this period in American history is crucial for understanding much of what has happened since then.

Many federal laws and other U.S. government actions during Reconstruction were intended to put African Americans on more equal footing with white citizens. The best-known changes were the 13th, 14th, and 15th amendments to the Constitution, which outlawed slavery, made African Americans into full-fledged citizens, and ensured voting rights for men who had previously been enslaved.

During Reconstruction, approximately two thousand African American men served as local, state, or national officials. Some of them were freemen before the war, and others — including John Roy Lynch — were freed only as a result of the conflict. Those who held office in the South were living symbols of the spread of freedom. Most notably, between 1870 and 1877, there were sixteen African Americans who served in the U.S. Congress from former Confederate states.

But there were only six more who served between 1878 and 1901. And between 1902 and 1972, there were zero.

What happened?

Put simply, white Southerners resisted and then reversed — through legislation and violence — the extension of freedom to their black neighbors. And as Reconstruction neared its end, the U.S. government did not keep up its efforts to protect its African American citizens in those states. It wasn't until the civil rights movement of the 1950s and 1960s that the nation's course was put right, back toward equality.

There have been tremendous gains in the decades since, but setbacks continue. It has taken us far longer to get to where we are today than John Roy Lynch would have imagined during the amazing age when a teenage slave could become a U.S. Congressman in just ten years' time.

TIMELINE

**The main events in John Roy Lynch's life appear in black.
State and national events are in red.**

1847   John Roy Lynch is born on September 10 at Tacony Plantation near Vidalia, Louisiana.

1850s   After his father's death, serves as a house slave at Dunleith Plantation, Alfred V. Davis's estate in the city of Natchez, Mississippi.

1860   Abraham Lincoln is elected President of the United States.

1861   Mississippi, Louisiana, and nine other slave states secede from the Union and form the Confederate States of America. The Civil War begins.

1862   Sent back to Tacony to work in the fields.

1863   President Lincoln issues the Emancipation Proclamation. Union troops occupy Natchez and Vidalia, freeing John Roy and other slaves.

     President Lincoln announces plans to restore the Confederate states to the Union after the war through a process of "Reconstruction."

1865   The U.S. government creates the Freedmen's Bureau to educate, protect, and support formerly enslaved people.

     On April 9, the Confederacy surrenders, ending the Civil War.

     On April 14, President Lincoln is shot. He dies the following day.

     Mississippi enacts "Black Codes," severely curtailing the freedom of African Americans.

1866   Congress passes the Civil Rights Act of 1866 and the 14th Amendment to the U.S. Constitution. These strike down the Black Codes and establish the citizenship of African Americans.

     The Ku Klux Klan is formed and soon begins its efforts to control African Americans through violence and intimidation.

1867   Becomes an active member and speaker in a Natchez Republican club.

     Congress declares that former Confederate states will be readmitted to the Union only after they have ratified the 14th Amendment and given African American men the right to vote.

1868   Campaigns for a new Mississippi constitution allowing African American men to vote.

     Amid threats of Klan violence, the new Mississippi constitution is rejected.

     After ratification by three-fourths of the states, the 14th Amendment becomes law. Several former Confederate states — but not yet Mississippi — return to the Union.

     Former Union general Adelbert Ames is appointed governor of Mississippi.

1868	African American men in the reconstructed states vote in a national election for the first time. Former Union general Ulysses S. Grant is elected President.
1869	Congress approves the 15th Amendment, which ensures male African American citizens' right to vote.
	Appointed by Governor Ames as justice of the peace for Natchez.
	Mississippi voters approve the new state constitution and the 14th and 15th Amendments to the U.S. Constitution, allowing the state to be readmitted to the Union.
	Elected to Mississippi's House of Representatives.
1870	The Mississippi legislature establishes schools for both black and white children. The Klan responds by attacking teachers and destroying schools.
1871	Approximately thirty African Americans are murdered in a Klan-led riot in Meridian, Mississippi. Congress passes the Ku Klux Klan Act to prosecute terrorists violating Constitutional rights.
1872	Elected Speaker of Mississippi's House of Representatives.
	The U.S. government shuts down the Freedmen's Bureau.
	Later that year, elected to the U.S. House of Representatives at age 25.
1873	The nation enters a financial crisis in which thousands of companies go out of business.
1874	The House of Representatives begins debating the Civil Rights Bill, which would ban discrimination against African Americans by railroads and hotels.
	As many as three hundred African Americans are murdered near Vicksburg, Mississippi, in a conflict with armed whites.
1875	Makes his "land of the free and the home of the brave" speech in support of the Civil Rights Bill, which becomes law but includes no means for enforcement.
	Narrowly re-elected to his House seat, though elsewhere in Mississippi elections are plagued by violence, intimidation, and fraud.
1876	Defeated in his campaign for a third Congressional term.
1877	Reconstruction ends when President Rutherford B. Hayes removes the few remaining federal troops tasked with upholding the law in former Confederate states.
1883	The U.S. Supreme Court strikes down the Civil Rights Act of 1875. In the years that follow, the South enacts "Jim Crow" laws that strip away the voting rights and other freedoms of black citizens.
1884	Marries Ella Somerville; they have one daughter and divorce in 1900.
1898	Serves as a major in the U.S. Army during the Spanish-American War.
1912	Having sold his land in Mississippi, moves to Chicago with new wife Cora Williamson Lynch.
1913	Writes *The Facts of Reconstruction* to correct racist distortions put forth by white historians.
1915	*The Birth of a Nation*, a Hollywood film misrepresenting Reconstruction and glorifying the Klan, becomes wildly popular and warps Americans' views of history for generations to come.
1939	John Roy Lynch dies on November 2 in Chicago. At the time of his death, he is working on his autobiography, which would be published in 1970 as *Reminiscences of an Active Life*.

AUTHOR'S NOTE

I don't imagine I'll ever tire of describing this book, as I have many times, by saying, "It's the story of a guy who in ten years went from teenage field slave to U.S. Congressman." That description astounds people. Even writing those words now, I marvel at the journey that John Roy Lynch made in such a short time, and at the fact that the opportunity ever existed for anyone to make that particular transformation.

Yet I also marvel at how little we Americans as a whole know about the period in which that opportunity came along — about Reconstruction, how it failed, and the consequences of that failure. This cultural blind spot makes me sad. I think it's a shame how little we question why the civil rights movement in this country occurred a full century following the emancipation of the slaves rather than immediately afterward. Based on the common knowledge of young and old alike, you would think that nothing of importance occurred between the assassination of Abraham Lincoln and the Wright brothers' first flight at Kitty Hawk nearly forty years later.

But then we stumble upon a story such as John Roy Lynch's. His is a personal tale so unlikely that it calls on us to linger, to ask questions, to seek to understand the context, and to delve into the details of the overlooked time in which he lived. During those stretches of history that textbooks and popular lore are content to rush through or gloss over, it's the individual sagas that grab us and remind us that here, too, is a fascinating period worth exploring — worth learning from and taking to heart and pondering how it applies to all we (think we) know of what came after.

There are more amazing ages in our past than you might expect. Here's to your discovery of them.

— *Chris Barton*

ILLUSTRATOR'S NOTE

I'm ashamed to admit that before illustrating *The Amazing Age of John Roy Lynch*, I wasn't very knowledgeable about Reconstruction. That bit of American history was like a puzzle to me, one that I'd never quite put together. While I was familiar with some of the pieces — Black Codes, lynchings, the Ku Klux Klan — there were other pieces I didn't know about. I needed to do some research in order to form a bigger picture.

I began my research by reading Lynch's autobiography, *Reminiscences of an Active Life*. I also watched documentaries on the Reconstruction era. I studied historical archives on the internet. I even visited the Old Capitol in Jackson, Mississippi, where John Roy Lynch once served as the Speaker of the House of Representatives. Some of what I learned horrified me. But I also felt a sense of pride at the resilience of African American people. We are survivors.

Visually, the story presented a few challenges. The end of the Civil War and the emancipation of enslaved people promised bright opportunities. But oftentimes, darkness was delivered instead. Southern whites were hostile to the idea of treating their former slaves as equals. Reconstruction was a violent time. Chris Barton was honest in telling Lynch's story; he did not sugarcoat history. Neither would I.

For the illustrations in this book, I used a rather childlike, naive style of art — even whimsical, though the serious subject matter of the book might belie such a description. My hope was that a more lighthearted style of artwork would be the best approach to introducing young readers to the harsh realities of Lynch's world, while also maintaining the dignity of African American people and their struggles.

I hope readers will be as inspired by John Roy Lynch's story as I am.

— *Don Tate*

FOR FURTHER READING

Bolden, Tonya. *Cause: Reconstruction America, 1863–1877*. New York: Alfred A. Knopf, 2005.

Greene, Meg. *Into the Land of Freedom: African Americans in Reconstruction*. Minneapolis: Lerner, 2004.

Hakim, Joy. *A History of US: Reconstructing America 1865–1890*. New York: Oxford University Press, 2006.

Hansen, Joyce. *"Bury Me Not in a Land of Slaves": African-Americans in the Time of Reconstruction*. Danbury, CT: Franklin Watts, 2000.

McPherson, James M. *Into the West: From Reconstruction to the Final Days of the American Frontier*. New York: Atheneum Books for Young Readers, 2006.

Mettger, Zak. *Reconstruction: America After the Civil War*. New York: Dutton, 1994.

Osborne, Linda Barrett. *Traveling the Freedom Road: From Slavery & the Civil War Through Reconstruction*. New York: Abrams Books for Young Readers, 2009.

Rappaport, Doreen. *Free At Last! Stories and Songs of Emancipation*. Illus. Shane W. Evans. Somerville, MA: Candlewick, 2004.

Ruggiero, Adriane. *Reconstruction*. New York: Marshall Cavendish, 2006.

For more about the research and writing of *The Amazing Age of John Roy Lynch*, visit **www.chrisbarton.info**.

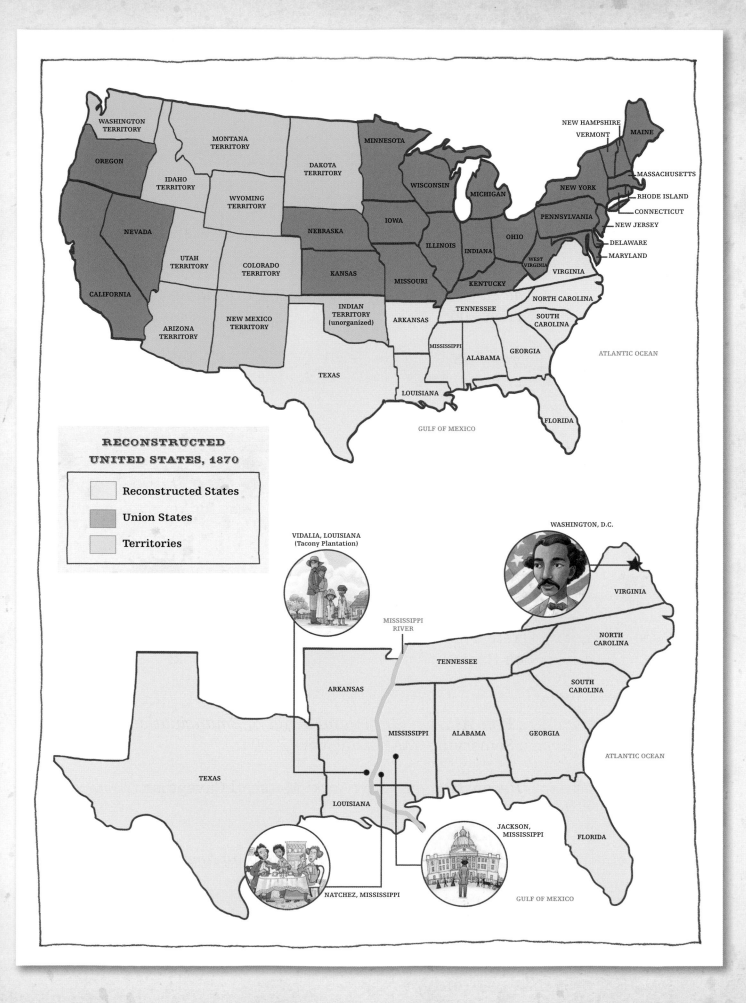

RECONSTRUCTED
UNITED STATES, 1870

Reconstructed States

Union States

Territories

WASHINGTON TERRITORY

OREGON

IDAHO TERRITORY

MONTANA TERRITORY

DAKOTA TERRITORY

MINNESOTA

WISCONSIN

MICHIGAN

NEW HAMPSHIRE

VERMONT

MAINE

NEW YORK

MASSACHUSETTS

RHODE ISLAND

CONNECTICUT

NEW JERSEY

PENNSYLVANIA

NEVADA

WYOMING TERRITORY

NEBRASKA

IOWA

ILLINOIS

INDIANA

OHIO

DELAWARE

MARYLAND

WEST VIRGINIA

VIRGINIA

CALIFORNIA

UTAH TERRITORY

COLORADO TERRITORY

KANSAS

MISSOURI

KENTUCKY

TENNESSEE

NORTH CAROLINA

ARIZONA TERRITORY

NEW MEXICO TERRITORY

INDIAN TERRITORY (unorganized)

ARKANSAS

SOUTH CAROLINA

MISSISSIPPI

ALABAMA

GEORGIA

ATLANTIC OCEAN

TEXAS

LOUISIANA

FLORIDA

GULF OF MEXICO

VIDALIA, LOUISIANA
(Tacony Plantation)

WASHINGTON, D.C.

MISSISSIPPI RIVER

VIRGINIA

NORTH CAROLINA

TENNESSEE

ARKANSAS

SOUTH CAROLINA

MISSISSIPPI

ALABAMA

GEORGIA

ATLANTIC OCEAN

TEXAS

LOUISIANA

JACKSON, MISSISSIPPI

FLORIDA

NATCHEZ, MISSISSIPPI

GULF OF MEXICO